Neuro Linguistic Programming

Unlock the Power of Your Mind

By Dylan Williamson

Index

Chapter 1. Introduction to NLP

- Definition and history of NLP
- Key principles and concepts of NLP
- The NLP communication model

Chapter 2. Representational Systems

- The five senses and how they affect communication
- How to identify and utilize a person's preferred representational system

Chapter 3. Language Patterns

- The structure of language and how it impacts our thoughts and behaviors
- Techniques for using language to influence and persuade others

Chapter 4. Anchoring

- Definition and explanation of anchoring
- Techniques for creating and utilizing anchors

Chapter 5. Submodalities

- Definition and explanation of submodalities
- Techniques for modifying and altering submodalities to change thoughts and behaviors

Chapter 6. Strategies

- Definition and explanation of strategies
- Techniques for identifying and utilizing strategies in communication and problem-solving

Chapter 7. Applications of NLP

- Using NLP in business
- Using NLP in leadership
- Using NLP in personal development
- Using NLP is relationships
- Using NLP in coaching
- Using NLP in therapy

Chapter 8. Advanced NLP Techniques

- Reframing and refocusing
- Parts integration and conflict resolution
- Time-line therapy and future pacing

Chapter 9. Ethics and Best Practices

- Ethical considerations in the use of NLP
- Best practices for using NLP with clients and in personal development

Chapter 10. Conclusion and Next Steps

- Review of key concepts and techniques learned
- Skills that complement NLP

Chapter 1

Introduction to NLP

Definition and History of NLP

Neuro-Linguistic Programming (NLP) is a discipline that combines the study of language, behavior, and the workings of the mind. It is a holistic approach to personal development and communication that has gained popularity in recent years, particularly in the fields of psychology, coaching, and therapy.
The history of NLP can be traced back to the 1970s, when Richard Bandler, a computer science student, and John Grinder, a linguistics professor, began studying successful therapists and communicators in order to uncover the underlying principles of their success. The two noticed that these individuals seemed to share certain patterns in their language and behavior, and they began to develop NLP as a way to codify and replicate these patterns.

One of the key concepts in NLP is the idea that our thoughts and behaviors are closely connected to the words we use and the sensory experiences we have. This means that by changing the way we use language and process information through our five senses, we can change our thoughts and behaviors. NLP practitioners aim to understand the unique ways in which each person experiences and processes information, in order to help them achieve their goals and overcome any limitations.

NLP is often compared to cognitive-behavioral therapy (CBT) and other forms of therapy that focus on changing thought patterns and behaviors. However, NLP is unique in its focus on language and sensory experiences as the key drivers of change. Practitioners use a variety of techniques, such as reframing and refocusing, anchoring, and submodality shifting, to help individuals gain new perspectives and make positive changes.

One of the key benefits of NLP is that it can be applied in a wide range of settings, from personal development to business and leadership. NLP has been used to help individuals overcome phobias, improve their communication skills, and increase their confidence and self-esteem. It has also been used to help organizations improve their teamwork, customer service, and overall effectiveness.

Despite its popularity, NLP has faced criticism from some in the scientific community who question its validity and effectiveness. However, proponents of NLP argue that it is a valuable tool for personal growth and that its benefits are supported by a growing body of research.

In conclusion, NLP is a discipline that combines the study of language, behavior, and the workings of the mind. It was developed in the 1970s as a way to codify and replicate the patterns of successful therapists and communicators. NLP practitioners aim to understand the unique ways in which each person experiences and processes information, in order to help them achieve their goals and overcome any limitations. Whether or not NLP is a scientifically valid discipline, it is clear that it has had a significant impact on personal development and communication and will likely continue to be a popular field for years to come.

Key Principles of NLP

Neuro-Linguistic Programming (NLP) is a discipline that focuses on the connection between language, behavior, and the workings of the mind. The key principles of NLP can be distilled into several core ideas that form the foundation of the discipline.
The first key principle of NLP is the idea that our thoughts and behaviors are closely connected to the words we use and the sensory experiences we have. NLP practitioners believe that by changing the way we use language and process information through our five senses, we can change our thoughts and behaviors. This means that NLP is a holistic approach to personal development and communication that considers the impact of language, sensory experiences, and mental processes on our thoughts and behaviors.
A second key principle of NLP is the idea of rapport. NLP practitioners believe that building rapport with others is critical to effective communication and relationship building. Rapport refers to the sense of connection and understanding between two or more individuals. NLP practitioners use a variety of techniques, such as mirroring and matching, to build rapport and establish a sense of connection with others.

A third key principle of NLP is the idea of reframing and refocusing. NLP practitioners believe that by changing the way we think about our experiences, we can change the impact they have on us. Reframing involves looking at a situation from a different perspective, while refocusing involves redirecting our attention to more positive and empowering thoughts. These techniques are used to help individuals overcome limiting beliefs and negative thought patterns, and to develop a more positive and empowering outlook on life.

A fourth key principle of NLP is the idea of anchoring. Anchoring refers to the process of associating a specific sensory experience or thought with a particular trigger, such as a word or gesture. NLP practitioners believe that by creating positive anchors, individuals can access positive states of mind and emotions whenever they need to. Anchors can be used to help individuals overcome negative emotions, such as anxiety or fear, and to build confidence and motivation.

A fifth key principle of NLP is the idea of submodalities. Submodalities refer to the specific ways in which we experience our thoughts and feelings. NLP practitioners believe that by changing the way we experience our thoughts and feelings, we can change the impact they have on us. For example, if we imagine a negative thought as being in black and white, we can change it to be in color, which will make the thought less intense and less impactful.

A final key principle of NLP is the idea of strategies. Strategies refer to the mental processes we use to achieve our goals and make decisions. NLP practitioners believe that by understanding the strategies we use, we can improve our decision-making and problem-solving skills, and achieve our goals more effectively. NLP practitioners use a variety of techniques, such as strategy elicitation and strategy installation, to help individuals understand and improve their strategies.

In conclusion, the key principles of NLP are based on the connection between language, behavior, and the workings of the mind. NLP practitioners believe that by changing the way we use language and process information, and by building rapport, reframing and refocusing, anchoring, and improving our strategies, we can change our thoughts and behaviors and achieve our goals. Whether or not NLP is a scientifically valid discipline, its principles have been found to be helpful by many individuals and organizations, and it will likely continue to be a popular field for years to come.

The NLP Communication Model

The NLP Communication Model is a fundamental concept in Neuro-Linguistic Programming (NLP) that explains how communication works and how we can use language to influence our thoughts and behaviors. The model is based on the idea that we process information through our five senses (sight, sound, touch, taste, and smell), and that our thoughts and behaviors are closely connected to the words we use and the sensory experiences we have.

The first component of the NLP Communication Model is our internal representation system, which is the way in which we process information through our five senses. Our internal representation system determines how we process information, and it can be visual, auditory, kinesthetic, olfactory, or gustatory. Understanding our own internal representation system, as well as the internal representation systems of others, is critical to effective communication.

The second component of the NLP Communication Model is our language system, which refers to the words and phrases we use to describe our experiences and thoughts. Our language system provides a window into our internal representation system, and it can be used to change the way we think and feel about our experiences. For example, if we describe a situation as being "overwhelming," we are more likely to experience it as such. However, if we describe the same situation as being "challenging," we are more likely to approach it with a sense of excitement and motivation.

The third component of the NLP Communication Model is our behavior system, which refers to the actions and physical responses we have in response to our thoughts and experiences. Our behavior system is closely connected to our internal representation system and language system, and it can be used to communicate our thoughts and experiences to others. For example, if we are nervous, our body may respond with physical symptoms, such as sweating or shaking, which can communicate our nervousness to others.

The NLP Communication Model also includes the idea of rapport, which is the sense of connection and understanding between two or more individuals. Building rapport is critical to effective communication, and NLP practitioners use a variety of techniques, such as mirroring and matching, to build rapport and establish a sense of connection with others.

Another important concept in the NLP Communication Model is reframing, which involves looking at a situation from a different perspective. Reframing can be used to change the way we think about our experiences and to overcome limiting beliefs and negative thought patterns. For example, if we are struggling with a difficult task, we can reframe our thoughts about it as an opportunity for growth and learning, which can help us approach the task with a more positive attitude.

Finally, the NLP Communication Model includes the idea of anchoring, which refers to the process of associating a specific sensory experience or thought with a particular trigger, such as a word or gesture. Anchoring can be used to help individuals access positive states of mind and emotions whenever they need to. For example, if we associate a certain song with feelings of happiness and excitement, we can listen to that song whenever we need to boost our mood.

In conclusion, the NLP Communication Model is a fundamental concept in NLP that explains how communication works and how we can use language to influence our thoughts and behaviors. By understanding our internal representation system, language system, behavior system, and the role of rapport, reframing, and anchoring, we can improve our communication skills and achieve our goals more effectively. Whether or not NLP is a scientifically valid discipline, its principles have been found to be helpful by many individuals and organizations, and it will likely continue to be a popular field for years to come.

Chapter 2

Representational systems

The Five Senses and How they Affect Communication

The five senses, which are sight, sound, touch, taste, and smell, play a critical role in how we communicate and perceive the world around us. Understanding how the five senses influence our communication can help us to be more effective communicators and to better understand the perspectives and experiences of others.

Sight, or visual processing, is often the dominant sense in our communication. Visual information is processed quickly and easily, and it is often used to form our first impressions of people and situations. When we communicate, we use visual cues, such as body language and facial expressions, to convey meaning and to build rapport. Additionally, visual information can be used to trigger emotions and memories, and it can be used to create a strong impact in advertising and other forms of media.

Sound, or auditory processing, is also an important aspect of communication. Our voice, tone, and inflection can convey meaning and convey our emotional state, even when we are not speaking. Additionally, the sound of our environment, such as music, can influence our emotions and can be used to create a certain mood or atmosphere.

Touch, or kinesthetic processing, is related to physical sensations and experiences. Touch is often used in communication to convey a sense of closeness and connection, such as in a handshake or hug. Touch can also be used to communicate emotional states, such as a pat on the back to express encouragement or a hug to convey comfort.

Taste and smell, or gustatory and olfactory processing, are less commonly used in communication but are still important in creating a sense of atmosphere and setting the mood. For example, the smell of freshly baked cookies can evoke feelings of comfort and nostalgia, while the taste of a bitter food can evoke feelings of displeasure.

It is important to understand that individuals have different preferences for the different senses and that some individuals are more visual, auditory, kinesthetic, olfactory, or gustatory in their processing than others. This means that some individuals may respond better to visual stimuli, while others may respond better to auditory or kinesthetic stimuli. Understanding an individual's preferred sense can help us to communicate more effectively with them and to understand their perspective.

In conclusion, the five senses play a critical role in our communication and how we perceive the world around us. By understanding the role of each of the five senses in communication, we can improve our ability to connect with others and to effectively convey our thoughts, feelings, and ideas. Whether we are communicating in business, relationships, or other areas of life, understanding the five senses and how they affect communication can help us to be more successful and to achieve our goals.

How to identify and utilize a person's preferred representational system

Representational systems, also known as modalities, are the ways in which we process information and represent our thoughts, feelings, and experiences. In Neuro-Linguistic Programming (NLP), it is believed that individuals have preferred representational systems, or ways in which they process information that are unique to them. Identifying and utilizing a person's preferred representational system can greatly enhance the effectiveness of communication.

There are five primary representational systems in NLP: visual, auditory, kinesthetic, olfactory, and gustatory. Visual individuals tend to process information primarily through their sight and are often described as visual thinkers. Auditory individuals tend to process information primarily through their hearing and are often described as auditory thinkers. Kinesthetic individuals tend to process information primarily through their physical sensations and are often described as feeling-oriented thinkers. Olfactory individuals tend to process information primarily through their sense of smell and are often described as smell-oriented thinkers. Gustatory individuals tend to process information primarily through their sense of taste and are often described as taste-oriented thinkers.

To identify a person's preferred representational system, there are several techniques that can be used. One of the most straightforward methods is to simply observe the person's language patterns. People often use words that are indicative of their preferred representational system when they are speaking. For example, a visual person may use phrases such as "I see what you're saying," "I picture that in my mind," or "I get a clear picture of that." An auditory person may use phrases such as "I hear you," "I listen to that," or "I can hear what you're saying." A kinesthetic person may use phrases such as "I feel that," "I touch that," or "I can feel it in my bones." An olfactory person may use phrases such as "I smell that," "I get a whiff of that," or "I can smell it in the air." A gustatory person may use phrases such as "I taste that," "I savor that," or "I can taste it in my mouth."

Another technique for identifying a person's preferred representational system is to pay attention to their body language. Visual individuals tend to look up and to the right, auditory individuals tend to look up and to the left, kinesthetic individuals tend to look down and to the right, olfactory individuals tend to look down and to the left, and gustatory individuals tend to look straight ahead. This pattern may not be consistent for every individual, but it can be a useful tool for identifying a person's preferred representational system.

Once a person's preferred representational system has been identified, it is important to utilize it when communicating with them. This can be done by speaking in a way that is consistent with their preferred representational system. For example, if a person is visual, it may be helpful to use visual language when communicating with them. This could involve using visual analogies or metaphors, or it could involve using visual aids, such as graphs or diagrams, to help illustrate your point. If a person is auditory, it may be helpful to use auditory language, such as using musical analogies or sound effects to help illustrate your point. If a person is kinesthetic, it may be helpful to use physical gestures or touch to help convey your message.

It is also important to consider a person's preferred representational system when choosing the environment in which to communicate. For example, a visual person may prefer to communicate in a visually stimulating environment, such as a room with lots of natural light or a room with colorful decorations. An auditory person may prefer to communicate in a quiet environment with minimal distractions, while a kinesthetic person may prefer to communicate while moving around, such as taking a walk or engaging in some physical activity. Understanding and utilizing a person's preferred representational system can help to create a more effective and meaningful connection, and can lead to more successful communication.

It is important to note that while a person may have a preferred representational system, they are still able to process information through all of the modalities. In other words, a visual person may still be able to hear and feel information, they simply prefer to process information through their visual system. It is also important to be flexible and adaptable, as a person's preferred representational system may change based on the situation or context.

In conclusion, the representational systems in NLP provide a framework for understanding how people process information and represent their thoughts and experiences. Identifying and utilizing a person's preferred representational system can greatly enhance the effectiveness of communication, and can lead to more meaningful and successful connections. It is important to be flexible and adaptable, and to consider the individual's preferred representational system in the context of the situation and environment. With a deeper understanding of the representational systems, it is possible to communicate in a way that is more effective, persuasive, and meaningful.

Chapter 3

Language Patterns

The Structure of language and how it impacts our thoughts and behaviors

The structure of language plays a crucial role in shaping our thoughts and behaviors. According to the principles of Neuro-Linguistic Programming (NLP), language is not just a means of communication, but also a tool for shaping our internal experiences and the way we interact with the world around us. Understanding the structure of language and how it impacts our thoughts and behaviors is an important aspect of NLP.

One of the key principles of NLP is that the way we use language is closely tied to the way we experience and process information. The words we choose, the tone of our voice, and the way we structure our sentences all influence our internal experiences and shape our thoughts and behaviors. For example, if we repeatedly use words that are associated with negative emotions, such as "fear" or "anxiety," we may start to experience those emotions more frequently. On the other hand, if we use words that are associated with positive emotions, such as "happiness" or "gratitude," we may start to experience those emotions more frequently as well.

The structure of language also plays a role in shaping our thoughts and behaviors by influencing the way we categorize and process information. For example, the way we use language to describe a situation can affect our perception of it. If we describe a situation as a "problem," we may approach it in a more negative and confrontational way, while if we describe the same situation as a "challenge," we may approach it in a more positive and solution-focused way. This highlights the importance of choosing our words carefully and being mindful of the language we use to describe our experiences.

Another important aspect of the structure of language is the way we use it to create and reinforce limiting beliefs. Our beliefs and values shape our perceptions and influence the way we behave, and the language we use can help to solidify these beliefs. For example, if we repeatedly use language that reinforces the belief that we are not good enough, we may start to behave in ways that are consistent with this belief, and it may become more ingrained over time. On the other hand, if we use language that reinforces positive beliefs and values, such as a belief in our own abilities or the belief that we can achieve our goals, we may start to behave in ways that are consistent with these beliefs and values.

In NLP, it is believed that our internal experiences are represented in a neurological format, which is influenced by the structure of our language. This means that the words we choose, the tone of our voice, and the way we structure our sentences can all have a profound impact on our thoughts and behaviors. By understanding the structure of language and how it influences our experiences, we can use language in a more effective way to shape our thoughts and behaviors in positive ways.

One of the ways in which we can use language to shape our thoughts and behaviors is by using positive affirmations. Positive affirmations are short, positive statements that we repeat to ourselves regularly. These affirmations can help to counteract negative self-talk and reinforce positive beliefs and values. For example, if we are feeling low and believe that we are not good enough, we can use positive affirmations such as "I am worthy and deserving of love and respect" or "I am capable and strong." By repeating these affirmations regularly, we can start to experience a shift in our thoughts and behaviors, and our negative beliefs may start to lose their grip on us. In conclusion, the structure of language plays a crucial role in shaping our thoughts and behaviors. The way we use language to describe our experiences, the language we use to reinforce our beliefs and values, and the way we structure our sentences can all have a profound impact on our internal experiences. By understanding the structure of language and how it influences our thoughts and behaviors, we can use language in a more effective and empowering way. This can include using positive affirmations, choosing our words carefully, and being mindful of the language we use to describe our experiences. By doing so, we can shape our thoughts and behaviors in positive and productive ways, and improve our overall well-being and happiness.

It is also important to recognize that the structure of language is culturally specific and varies from one language to another. Understanding the cultural nuances and differences in language can help us to communicate more effectively with people from different cultures, and avoid misunderstandings and misinterpretations.

In summary, the structure of language plays a critical role in shaping our thoughts and behaviors. By understanding the structure of language and how it influences our experiences, we can use language in a more effective and empowering way, and improve our overall well-being and happiness.

Techniques for using language to influence and persuade others

Language is a powerful tool that can be used to influence and persuade others. Understanding the techniques for using language effectively can help you to communicate more effectively and achieve your goals. In this article, we will discuss some of the key techniques for using language to influence and persuade others, based on the principles of Neuro-Linguistic Programming (NLP).

Matching and mirroring

One of the most effective techniques for using language to influence and persuade others is matching and mirroring. This involves mirroring the other person's language, tone of voice, and body language. By doing this, you create rapport and build trust with the other person, which makes it easier to persuade them. For example, if the other person speaks slowly and calmly, you should speak slowly and calmly as well. If the other person uses a lot of hand gestures, you should use hand gestures too. By matching and mirroring the other person, you are showing that you are attuned to their needs and that you understand and respect their point of view.

Using positive language

Another important technique for using language to influence and persuade others is to use positive language. This means using words and phrases that are associated with positive emotions and experiences, such as "exciting," "fun," and "rewarding." By using positive language, you can create a positive and optimistic atmosphere, which makes it easier to persuade others. Positive language can also help to build rapport and trust, and can make the other person feel more comfortable and relaxed.

Using hypothetical questions

Hypothetical questions are questions that begin with "what if" or "imagine." These types of questions can be very effective for influencing and persuading others because they allow the other person to experience a situation in their imagination. By doing this, they are more likely to understand and accept your point of view. For example, if you are trying to persuade someone to take a particular action, you could ask them, "What if you could achieve your goals more easily by taking this action?" This question allows the other person to imagine the positive outcomes of taking the action, which makes it more likely that they will be persuaded to take it.

Using story-telling

Stories are a powerful tool for influencing and persuading others because they allow you to communicate a message in an engaging and memorable way. By using stories, you can create an emotional connection with the other person, which makes it easier to persuade them. For example, if you are trying to persuade someone to adopt a particular point of view, you could tell them a story about someone who faced a similar situation and was able to achieve a positive outcome by adopting that point of view. This story can serve as a powerful motivator for the other person, making it more likely that they will be persuaded to adopt the same point of view.

Using analogies and metaphors
Analogies and metaphors can be very effective for influencing and persuading others because they help to make complex ideas more accessible and understandable. Analogies and metaphors are comparisons that are used to help explain a concept or idea. For example, you could use the analogy of a journey to explain the process of change, or you could use the metaphor of a seed to explain the process of growth. By using analogies and metaphors, you can help the other person to understand your point of view more easily and be more likely to be persuaded by it.
Using presuppositions
Presuppositions are statements or questions that assume a particular outcome or response. By using presuppositions, you can influence the other person's thoughts and behaviors in a subtle and indirect way. For example, if you are trying to persuade someone to take a particular action, you could ask a question that presupposes that they will take the action, such as "When will you be taking this action?" This question implies that the other person has already decided to take the action, and makes it more likely that they will actually take it.
Using non-verbal communication

In addition to using language to influence and persuade others, it is also important to pay attention to your non-verbal communication. This includes your body language, tone of voice, and facial expressions. Your non-verbal communication can have a big impact on how others perceive you and your message, and can be a powerful tool for influencing and persuading others. For example, if you use confident and assertive body language and a strong tone of voice, you are more likely to be perceived as credible and persuasive.

In conclusion, there are many techniques for using language to influence and persuade others, and by understanding these techniques, you can communicate more effectively and achieve your goals. Whether you are trying to persuade someone to take a particular action, adopt a particular point of view, or simply make a positive impression, using language effectively can make all the difference. Remember, the key to using language to influence and persuade others is to be aware of your own communication style, understand the communication style of the other person, and use language and non-verbal communication in a way that is appropriate for the situation.

Chapter 4

Anchoring

Definition and explanation of anchoring

Anchoring is a concept in neuro-linguistic programming (NLP) that refers to the idea that a person's thoughts and emotions can be influenced by specific stimuli, such as a word, a gesture, or a physical sensation. The idea is that once a person has experienced a particular state or emotion, they can be anchored to that state by a specific stimulus, and then be brought back to that state by the same stimulus at a later time. For example, imagine that you are feeling happy and relaxed after a vacation. You associate this happy and relaxed state with a specific gesture, such as a finger snap. The next time you feel stressed or upset, you can snap your fingers and be brought back to the happy and relaxed state you experienced on vacation. This is an example of anchoring.

Anchoring is thought to occur because the brain associates specific stimuli with specific emotions and experiences. When a person is anchored to a particular state, the brain becomes more likely to experience that state again in the future in response to the same stimulus. Anchoring is a way of influencing a person's thoughts and emotions, and it can be a powerful tool for changing negative thought patterns, improving emotional well-being, and achieving personal and professional goals.

There are several different types of anchoring, including sensory anchoring, self-anchoring, and environmental anchoring.

1. Sensory anchoring: Sensory anchoring is a type of anchoring that involves a specific physical sensation. For example, a person might associate a happy state with a certain touch or pressure on their arm, or a relaxed state with a certain temperature. Sensory anchoring can be especially effective because physical sensations are very real and powerful, and they can have a profound impact on a person's thoughts and emotions.

2. Self-anchoring: Self-anchoring is a type of anchoring that involves a specific internal state, such as a feeling or thought. For example, a person might associate a confident state with a specific mental image or thought, such as imagining themselves as successful and in control. Self-anchoring can be a powerful way to change

negative thought patterns and improve self-confidence.

3. Environmental anchoring: Environmental anchoring involves associating a specific environment or location with a particular state. For example, a person might associate their home with feelings of peace and relaxation, and when they return home, they may feel more relaxed and at peace. Environmental anchoring can be a way to create positive associations with specific environments and improve overall well-being.

Anchoring can be a useful tool for improving personal and professional success. By anchoring positive states and emotions, a person can overcome negative thought patterns and improve their emotional well-being. Anchoring can also be used to increase motivation, focus, and productivity, and to achieve specific goals. For example, a salesperson might use anchoring to associate a confident and assertive state with a specific gesture or phrase, such as a fist pump or the phrase "I am confident and assertive." This can help the salesperson overcome any nervousness or self-doubt, and perform at their best during sales presentations.

It is important to note that anchoring should be used ethically and appropriately. The power of anchoring can be used for good or bad, and it is up to the individual to use it responsibly. If used in a manipulative or unethical manner, anchoring can have negative consequences and harm the individual being anchored.

In conclusion, anchoring is a concept in NLP that refers to the idea that a person's thoughts and emotions can be influenced by specific stimuli. There are several different types of anchoring, including sensory anchoring, self- anchoring, and environmental anchoring. By associating specific stimuli with specific states or emotions, a person can be anchored to those states, and be brought back to those states in the future by the same stimuli. Anchoring can be a powerful tool for changing negative thought patterns, improving emotional well-being, and achieving personal and professional goals.

Anchoring can be used in various ways, such as in sales, therapy, and self-help. In sales, for example, a salesperson might use anchoring to associate a confident and assertive state with a specific gesture or phrase, which can help them overcome nervousness and perform at their best during sales presentations. In therapy, anchoring can be used to help a person overcome negative thoughts and emotions, and improve their well-being. In self-help, anchoring can be used to improve motivation, focus, and productivity, and to achieve specific goals.

It is important to use anchoring ethically and appropriately, and to use it in a manner that benefits the individual being anchored. If used in a manipulative or unethical manner, anchoring can have negative consequences and harm the individual being anchored.

In summary, anchoring is a powerful tool for influencing a person's thoughts and emotions, and it can be used in various ways to improve personal and professional success. By using anchoring in an ethical and appropriate manner, a person can achieve their goals and improve their well-being.

Techniques for creating and utilizing anchors

Anchoring is a technique used in Neuro-Linguistic Programming (NLP) to link a specific thought, emotion, or state of mind to a specific trigger, such as a sound, gesture, or word. The trigger can then be used to recall that thought, emotion, or state of mind at a later time. This can be a powerful tool for improving motivation, enhancing emotional well-being, and increasing personal and professional success. In this article, we will discuss several techniques for creating and utilizing anchors in NLP.

Sensory-Based Anchoring: This technique involves creating an anchor by using one of the five senses: visual, auditory, kinesthetic, olfactory, and gustatory. For example, you might associate a positive emotion with a specific smell, or a confident state of mind with a particular sound. To create a sensory-based anchor, simply focus on the desired emotion or state, and then associate it with a specific sensory trigger.

Environmental Anchoring: This technique involves creating an anchor by associating a specific thought, emotion, or state of mind with a specific location or environment. For example, you might associate a relaxed state with a particular room in your home, or a confident state with your office. To create an environmental anchor, simply focus on the desired emotion or state, and then associate it with the specific location or environment.

Self-Anchoring: This technique involves creating an anchor by using your own body or movements as the trigger. For example, you might associate a confident state with a particular gesture, or a relaxed state with a specific breathing pattern. To create a self-anchor, simply focus on the desired emotion or state, and then associate it with a specific movement or body position.

Verbal Anchoring: This technique involves creating an anchor by using a specific word or phrase as the trigger. For example, you might associate a confident state with the phrase "I am confident," or a relaxed state with the word "relax." To create a verbal anchor, simply focus on the desired emotion or state, and then associate it with the specific word or phrase.

Once you have created an anchor, you can use it to recall the desired thought, emotion, or state at a later time. To do this, simply focus on the trigger, and allow yourself to be drawn back to the associated thought, emotion, or state. With practice, you will be able to access your anchors quickly and easily, and use them to achieve your goals.

It is important to use anchoring ethically and appropriately, and to use it in a manner that benefits the individual being anchored. If used in a manipulative or unethical manner, anchoring can have negative consequences and harm the individual being anchored.

In conclusion, anchoring is a powerful tool for influencing a person's thoughts and emotions, and there are several techniques for creating and utilizing anchors in NLP. By using these techniques in an ethical and appropriate manner, a person can improve their motivation, emotional well-being, and personal and professional success.

Sensory-based anchoring techniques

Sensory-based anchoring is a technique used in Neuro-Linguistic Programming (NLP) to associate a specific thought, emotion, or state of mind with a sensory trigger, such as a sound, gesture, or scent. This technique can be used to improve motivation, enhance emotional well-being, and increase personal and professional success. In this article, we will discuss how to create sensory-based anchors in NLP.

The first step in creating a sensory-based anchor is to identify the thought, emotion, or state of mind that you want to associate with the trigger. It can be helpful to think about a time when you felt that emotion or state of mind in a particularly strong way. Next, you will need to choose a sensory trigger that you can associate with that thought, emotion, or state.

There are five different types of sensory triggers: visual, auditory, kinesthetic, olfactory, and gustatory. Visual triggers include sights, such as colors or patterns. Auditory triggers include sounds, such as music or a specific voice. Kinesthetic triggers include physical sensations, such as touch or movement. Olfactory triggers include scents, such as perfume or essential oils. Gustatory triggers include tastes, such as sweet or sour flavors.

Once you have identified the thought, emotion, or state of mind that you want to associate with the trigger and chosen a type of sensory trigger, you can start the anchoring process. To create a sensory-based anchor, you need to focus on the thought, emotion, or state, and then associate it with the sensory trigger.

One way to do this is to imagine the thought, emotion, or state as a physical object, such as a ball. Hold the ball in your mind's eye, and then imagine tossing it to the sensory trigger. As you do this, you should also experience the thought, emotion, or state. Repeat this process several times until you have created a strong association between the thought, emotion, or state and the sensory trigger.

You can also use repetition to strengthen the association between the thought, emotion, or state and the sensory trigger. Repeat the anchoring process several times, each time focusing on the thought, emotion, or state and the sensory trigger. The more you repeat the process, the stronger the association will become.

Once you have created a sensory-based anchor, you can use it to recall the desired thought, emotion, or state at a later time. To do this, simply focus on the sensory trigger, and allow yourself to be drawn back to the associated thought, emotion, or state. With practice, you will be able to access your anchors quickly and easily, and use them to achieve your goals.

In conclusion, sensory-based anchoring is a powerful technique used in NLP to associate a specific thought, emotion, or state of mind with a sensory trigger. By focusing on the desired thought, emotion, or state and associating it with a sensory trigger, you can create a strong association that can be used to recall the thought, emotion, or state at a later time. With practice, you can use sensory-based anchors to improve your motivation, enhance your emotional well-being, and increase your personal and professional success.

Environment based anchoring techniques

Environment-based anchoring is a technique used in Neuro-Linguistic Programming (NLP) to associate a specific thought, emotion, or state of mind with a particular environment or setting. This type of anchoring can be useful for creating a sense of comfort, security, or confidence in a specific situation, and for building resilience in the face of stress and change. In this article, we will discuss how to create an environment-based anchor.

The first step in creating an environment-based anchor is to identify the thought, emotion, or state of mind that you want to associate with the environment. It can be helpful to think about a time when you felt that emotion or state of mind in a particularly strong way, and to identify the environment or setting in which you were at that time.

Next, you will need to focus on the thought, emotion, or state, and then associate it with the environment or setting. To do this, you can use your imagination to create a mental image of the environment, and then imagine yourself experiencing the thought, emotion, or state in that environment. You can also use visual or auditory triggers, such as colors, sounds, or music, to help you associate the thought, emotion, or state with the environment.

One way to do this is to imagine yourself in the environment, and then imagine the thought, emotion, or state as a physical object, such as a ball. Hold the ball in your mind's eye, and then imagine tossing it into the environment. As you do this, you should also experience the thought, emotion, or state. Repeat this process several times until you have created a strong association between the thought, emotion, or state and the environment.

You can also use repetition to strengthen the association between the thought, emotion, or state and the environment. Repeat the anchoring process several times, each time focusing on the thought, emotion, or state and the environment. The more you repeat the process, the stronger the association will become.

Once you have created an environment-based anchor, you can use it to recall the desired thought, emotion, or state at a later time. To do this, simply focus on the environment or setting, and allow yourself to be drawn back to the associated thought, emotion, or state. With practice, you will be able to access your anchors quickly and easily, and use them to achieve your goals.

In conclusion, environment-based anchoring is a powerful technique used in NLP to associate a specific thought, emotion, or state of mind with a particular environment or setting. By focusing on the desired thought, emotion, or state and associating it with an environment or setting, you can create a strong association that can be used to recall the thought, emotion, or state at a later time. With practice, you can use environment-based anchors to create a sense of comfort, security, or confidence in a specific situation, and to build resilience in the face of stress and change.

Self-anchoring techniques

Self-anchoring can be useful for creating a sense of confidence, motivation, or positive emotions in difficult situations, and for building resilience in the face of stress and change. In this article, we will discuss how to create a self-anchor. The first step in creating a self-anchor is to identify the thought, emotion, or state of mind that you want to associate with the physical gesture or sensation. It can be helpful to think about a time when you felt that emotion or state of mind in a particularly strong way, and to identify the physical gesture or sensation that you were experiencing at that time.

Next, you will need to focus on the thought, emotion, or state, and then associate it with the physical gesture or sensation. To do this, you can use your imagination to create a mental image of the physical gesture or sensation, and then imagine yourself experiencing the thought, emotion, or state at the same time. You can also use visual or auditory triggers, such as colors, sounds, or music, to help you associate the thought, emotion, or state with the physical gesture or sensation.

One way to do this is to imagine yourself in a situation where you are experiencing the thought, emotion, or state, and then imagine performing the physical gesture or sensation. As you do this, you should also experience the thought, emotion, or state. Repeat this process several times until you have created a strong association between the thought, emotion, or state and the physical gesture or sensation.

You can also use repetition to strengthen the association between the thought, emotion, or state and the physical gesture or sensation. Repeat the anchoring process several times, each time focusing on the thought, emotion, or state and the physical gesture or sensation. The more you repeat the process, the stronger the association will become.

Once you have created a self-anchor, you can use it to recall the desired thought, emotion, or state at a later time. To do this, simply perform the physical gesture or sensation, and allow yourself to be drawn back to the associated thought, emotion, or state. With practice, you will be able to access your self-anchors quickly and easily, and use them to achieve your goals. In conclusion, self-anchoring is a powerful technique used in NLP to associate a specific thought, emotion, or state of mind with a physical gesture or sensation. By focusing on the desired thought, emotion, or state and associating it with a physical gesture or sensation, you can create a strong association that can be used to recall the thought, emotion, or state at a later time. With practice, you can use self-anchors to create a sense of confidence, motivation, or positive emotions in difficult situations, and to build resilience in the face of stress and change.

Verbal Anchoring Techniques

Verbal anchoring can be useful for creating a sense of confidence, motivation, or positive emotions in difficult situations, and for building resilience in the face of stress and change. In this article, we will discuss how to create a verbal anchor.

The first step in creating a verbal anchor is to identify the thought, emotion, or state of mind that you want to associate with the word or phrase. It can be helpful to think about a time when you felt that emotion or state of mind in a particularly strong way, and to identify the word or phrase that you would associate with that experience.

Next, you will need to focus on the thought, emotion, or state, and then associate it with the word or phrase. To do this, you can use your imagination to create a mental image of the thought, emotion, or state, and then imagine yourself saying the word or phrase out loud. As you say the word or phrase, you should also experience the thought, emotion, or state.

You can also use repetition to strengthen the association between the thought, emotion, or state and the word or phrase. Repeat the anchoring process several times, each time focusing on the thought, emotion, or state and the word or phrase. The more you repeat the process, the stronger the association will become.

Once you have created a verbal anchor, you can use it to recall the desired thought, emotion, or state at a later time. To do this, simply say the word or phrase out loud, and allow yourself to be drawn back to the associated thought, emotion, or state. With practice, you will be able to access your verbal anchors quickly and easily, and use them to achieve your goals.

It is important to choose a word or phrase that is simple and easy to remember, and that you can say easily and quickly in any situation. You may also want to choose a word or phrase that is meaningful to you, and that you can associate with the desired thought, emotion, or state.

In conclusion, verbal anchoring is a powerful technique used in NLP to associate a specific thought, emotion, or state of mind with a word or phrase. By focusing on the desired thought, emotion, or state and associating it with a word or phrase, you can create a strong association that can be used to recall the thought, emotion, or state at a later time. With practice, you can use verbal anchors to create a sense of confidence, motivation, or positive emotions in difficult situations, and to build resilience in the face of stress and change.

Chapter 5

Submodalities

Submodalities are the specific sensory elements that make up our internal representations of the world. These elements include visual, auditory, kinesthetic, olfactory, and gustatory components, and they help us to distinguish between different experiences and memories. Understanding and manipulating submodalities is a key aspect of Neuro-Linguistic Programming (NLP), as these elements play a crucial role in shaping our thoughts, emotions, and behaviors.

Visual submodalities refer to the visual elements of our internal representations, such as the location, size, color, brightness, and clarity of an image. For example, an image of a childhood memory may be bright, clear, and large, while an image of a traumatic experience may be dark, blurry, and small.

Auditory submodalities refer to the sounds and voices we hear in our internal representations, including volume, tone, pace, and rhythm. For example, a pleasant memory may be accompanied by a soft, soothing voice, while an unpleasant memory may be accompanied by a loud, harsh voice.

Kinesthetic submodalities refer to the feelings and sensations we experience in our internal representations, such as pressure, temperature, and texture. For example, a memory of a warm summer day may be accompanied by a warm, sunny feeling, while a memory of a cold winter day may be accompanied by a cold, shivery feeling.

Olfactory and gustatory submodalities refer to the scents and tastes we experience in our internal representations. For example, a memory of a delicious meal may be accompanied by the taste and smell of the food, while a memory of a bad experience may be accompanied by an unpleasant scent or taste.

Each of these submodalities has the power to shape our thoughts, emotions, and behaviors. For example, changing the brightness and clarity of an image can change our perception of an experience, making it seem more or less positive. Similarly, changing the volume, tone, or pace of a voice can change the emotional impact of a memory.

In NLP, submodalities are used as a tool for personal change and improvement. By identifying and changing the submodalities of a particular thought, emotion, or behavior, individuals can reshape their experiences and perceptions, and create new and more desirable patterns of thinking and behavior.

One of the key techniques for working with submodalities is called submodality mapping. This involves comparing the submodalities of two experiences or memories and identifying the differences between them. For example, an individual may compare the submodalities of a positive memory with those of a negative memory, and identify the differences in the visual, auditory, kinesthetic, olfactory, and gustatory elements of each.

Once the differences have been identified, the individual can then modify the submodalities of the negative memory, making it more similar to the positive memory. This may involve changing the brightness and clarity of an image, increasing the volume and pace of a voice, or intensifying the warmth and sunny feeling associated with a positive memory.

Another technique for working with submodalities is called submodality testing. This involves testing the submodalities of a particular thought, emotion, or behavior, to determine which elements are the most powerful in shaping that experience. For example, an individual may test the volume, tone, and pace of a voice to determine which elements are most strongly associated with a particular thought, emotion, or behavior.

In conclusion, submodalities are the specific sensory elements that make up our internal representations of the world, and play a crucial role in shaping our thoughts, emotions, and behaviors. Understanding and manipulating submodalities is a key aspect of NLP, and can be used for personal change.

Techniques for modifying and altering submodalities to change thoughts and behaviors

In NLP, techniques for modifying and altering submodalities are used to change thoughts and behaviors. These techniques are based on the idea that by changing the way we represent information in our minds, we can change our thoughts, feelings, and behaviors. By working with submodalities, NLP practitioners aim to create new, empowering ways of thinking and being, and to replace old, limiting patterns.

One of the most commonly used techniques for modifying submodalities is called the Swish Pattern. This technique is used to help individuals quickly shift their focus from a negative thought or behavior to a positive one. The Swish Pattern works by using the power of visualization to create a new, more positive submodal representation of a particular experience.

To use the Swish Pattern, you first identify the negative thought or behavior you would like to change. Next, you imagine a vivid, positive image that represents the desired outcome. This image is then made as large and bright as possible, while the original negative thought is made small and dim. In a final step, the positive image "swishes" over the negative thought, replacing it and creating a new, positive submodal representation.

Another technique for modifying submodalities is the Reframing technique. Reframing involves changing the way we view a particular experience by altering its submodalities. For example, if someone is feeling anxious about a public speaking event, a reframing technique might involve imagining the experience from a different perspective, such as viewing it as an opportunity to share their knowledge and skills with others. By doing so, the individual's submodal representation of the experience changes, and the anxiety is reduced.

A third technique for modifying submodalities is the Re-imprinting technique. Re-imprinting is a more advanced NLP technique that works by modifying submodalities in a past memory, thereby changing the way it affects us in the present. The technique involves accessing a past memory, identifying any negative submodalities associated with it, and then changing those submodalities to create a more positive, empowering representation of the memory. By doing so, the individual is able to change their relationship to the past, and to the thoughts and behaviors that have been associated with it.

In conclusion, modifying and altering submodalities is a powerful tool for personal change and growth. By understanding how submodalities influence our thoughts, feelings, and behaviors, NLP practitioners are able to create new, empowering ways of thinking and being. Whether through the Swish Pattern, Reframing, or Re-imprinting, NLP techniques for modifying submodalities offer a valuable toolkit for anyone looking to make lasting and meaningful changes in their lives.

Chapter 6

Strategies

Definition and explanation of strategies

Neuro-Linguistic Programming (NLP) strategies are techniques that are used to achieve specific outcomes and to help individuals change the way they think and behave. NLP strategies are designed to be highly effective and to bring about lasting change, and they are based on the idea that our thoughts, feelings, and behaviors are interrelated and can be influenced by the way we represent information in our minds. One of the key principles of NLP is that our thoughts, feelings, and behaviors are represented in our minds through the use of sensory-based representations, or "representational systems." NLP strategies work by accessing and modifying these representational systems, and by creating new, empowering ways of thinking and being.

One common NLP strategy is called the Outcome Frame. The Outcome Frame is a powerful tool for setting goals and for creating a roadmap for achieving those goals. The technique involves identifying a specific outcome that you would like to achieve, and then breaking that outcome down into smaller, more manageable steps. By doing so, you are able to create a clear and actionable plan for achieving your desired outcome, and to focus your thoughts, feelings, and behaviors in a way that is aligned with your goal.

Another NLP strategy is called Reframing. Reframing is a technique for changing the way we view a particular experience or situation, and for creating a new, more positive perspective. Reframing works by accessing and modifying the representational systems associated with a particular experience or situation, and by creating a new, more empowering way of viewing that experience or situation. For example, if someone is feeling anxious about a public speaking event, a reframing technique might involve imagining the experience as an opportunity to share their knowledge and skills with others, rather than as a threat.

A third NLP strategy is called the Anchoring technique. Anchoring is a technique for creating a strong and immediate connection between a particular thought, feeling, or behavior, and a specific trigger, such as a sound, gesture, or word. Anchors is described in depth in the previous part. Return to part 5 for more information on anchoring.

In conclusion, NLP strategies are a set of powerful techniques for achieving specific outcomes and for changing the way we think and behave. Whether through the Outcome Frame, Reframing, or Anchoring, NLP strategies offer a valuable toolkit for anyone looking to make meaningful and lasting change in their lives. By accessing and modifying the representational systems that underlie our thoughts, feelings, and behaviors, NLP strategies help us to create new, empowering ways of thinking and being, and to replace old, limiting patterns.

Techniques for identifying and utilizing strategies in communication and problem-solving

Neuro-Linguistic Programming (NLP) is a powerful approach to communication and problem-solving that can help individuals achieve their goals and improve their relationships with others. NLP techniques are designed to help individuals understand and influence their own thoughts, feelings, and behaviors, as well as those of others.
One of the key techniques in NLP for identifying and utilizing strategies in communication and problem-solving is the Meta-Model. The Meta-Model is a set of language patterns that can be used to uncover the underlying assumptions and beliefs that drive an individual's thoughts, feelings, and behaviors. By using the Meta-Model, NLP practitioners can help individuals identify and change limiting beliefs and assumptions, and to create new, empowering ways of thinking and being.

Another NLP technique for identifying and utilizing strategies in communication and problem-solving is the Milton Model. The Milton Model is a set of language patterns that can be used to influence others and to create rapport and understanding. The Milton Model is particularly useful in situations where it is important to build trust and to establish a positive relationship, such as in sales, counseling, or conflict resolution.

A third NLP technique for identifying and utilizing strategies in communication and problem-solving is the Reframing technique. Reframing is a technique for changing the way we view a particular experience or situation, and for creating a new, more positive perspective. Reframing works by accessing and modifying the representational systems associated with a particular experience or situation, and by creating a new, more empowering way of viewing that experience or situation. For example, if someone is feeling anxious about a public speaking event, a reframing technique might involve imagining the experience as an opportunity to share their knowledge and skills with others, rather than as a threat.

One of the most important aspects of NLP is the use of rapport and rapport building techniques. Rapport is the process of establishing a relationship of mutual understanding and trust with another person. Rapport is an essential part of effective communication and problem-solving, and NLP provides a number of techniques for building and maintaining rapport, including matching and mirroring, calibration, and rapport-focused language patterns.

In conclusion, NLP provides a wealth of techniques for identifying and utilizing strategies in communication and problem-solving. Whether through the Meta-Model, the Milton Model, Reframing, or rapport building techniques, NLP offers a valuable toolkit for anyone looking to improve their communication skills and to achieve their goals in life. By understanding the underlying thought processes and beliefs that drive our behavior, NLP helps us to become more effective communicators, problem-solvers, and relationship builders, and to create positive change in our lives and in the lives of those around us.

Chapter 7

Applications of NLP

Using NLP in Business

Neuro-Linguistic Programming (NLP) is a powerful tool that can be used to improve communication, problem-solving, and leadership skills in the business world. NLP provides a framework for understanding how people process information and communicate, and offers techniques for adapting your communication style to match the needs of others.

One of the key principles of NLP is the understanding that everyone has a unique way of processing information, based on their own perspectives, values, and beliefs. This means that in order to communicate effectively and influence others, it is important to understand these differences and to adapt your approach accordingly.

In business, NLP can be used to improve communication with customers and clients, to negotiate more effectively, and to build stronger relationships with team members and colleagues. For example, NLP can help business leaders to identify the preferred communication style of each individual, whether it be visual, auditory, or kinesthetic, and to tailor their approach accordingly. This can help to build rapport and increase the chances of a successful outcome.

Another key aspect of NLP is the use of language to influence and persuade others. This can involve using specific language patterns and techniques, such as using metaphors and stories, to help people understand complex ideas and concepts. NLP can also be used to build rapport and trust, by using active listening and empathy, to understand the other person's point of view.

In terms of problem-solving, NLP can be used to help individuals and teams to identify and overcome obstacles and challenges, to create new and innovative solutions, and to develop a more positive and resourceful mindset. For example, NLP can be used to help individuals to reframe negative thoughts and beliefs, and to develop a more proactive and solution-focused approach to problem-solving.

NLP can also be used to improve leadership skills, by helping leaders to communicate their vision and goals more effectively, to create a sense of motivation and direction in their team, and to resolve conflicts in a constructive manner. For example, NLP can be used to help leaders to identify the underlying motivations and values of their team members, and to communicate in a way that speaks to those motivations. This can help to create a sense of engagement and buy-in, and to build stronger relationships with team members.

Another important aspect of NLP is the use of techniques for modifying and altering submodalities, or the specific qualities and attributes of our internal representations of experiences. By changing the submodalities of our thoughts and experiences, we can change the way we feel and behave, and overcome limiting beliefs and habits.

In conclusion, NLP offers a range of powerful techniques that can be applied in the business world to improve communication, problem-solving, and leadership skills. By understanding the subjective nature of people's experiences and using language to influence and persuade, NLP can help individuals and organizations to achieve their goals and to create positive change.

Using NLP in Leadership

Neuro-Linguistic Programming (NLP) is a field that has gained popularity in recent years for its potential to help individuals and organizations improve their communication, relationships, and performance. In particular, NLP has been found to be an effective tool for leaders looking to improve their leadership style and effectiveness. Therefore, we will examine how NLP can be used in leadership and why it is becoming a popular tool for leaders.

First, let's examine what NLP is and how it works. NLP is a method of exploring how people think and communicate, based on the idea that our thoughts, feelings, and behaviors are interconnected. NLP practitioners use techniques such as language patterns, visualizations, and anchoring to help individuals understand their thought processes and change negative thought patterns. NLP techniques are designed to help individuals understand and influence their own thoughts and behaviors, as well as those of others.

One of the key principles of NLP is that the way people communicate can reveal a lot about their thought processes, beliefs, and motivations. For example, the language someone uses can indicate the type of thought process they are in, such as visual, auditory, or kinesthetic. NLP practitioners use this information to help individuals understand their thought patterns and change them if needed.

In leadership, NLP can be used to help leaders understand their own communication style and how it affects their team. For example, a leader who has a tendency to be overly critical may be seen as negative and may have a negative impact on the team's morale. Using NLP techniques, the leader can become more aware of their language and behavior patterns and change them to be more positive and supportive.

Another way NLP can be used in leadership is to help leaders understand their team members. By understanding how different team members process information and communicate, leaders can tailor their communication style to best suit each team member, improving overall communication and team dynamics.

NLP can also be used to help leaders overcome limiting beliefs and negative thought patterns. For example, a leader who has a belief that they are not a good public speaker may struggle with giving presentations or leading meetings. NLP techniques can be used to help the leader understand and change this limiting belief, allowing them to become a more effective communicator.

One of the benefits of using NLP in leadership is that it can help leaders become more flexible in their communication style. By understanding the different ways people process information, leaders can adapt their communication style to best suit each individual they are communicating with. This can help improve relationships with team members and other stakeholders, leading to more positive outcomes.

In conclusion, NLP is a valuable tool for leaders looking to improve their communication style and effectiveness. By understanding their own communication style and how it affects others, leaders can become more effective communicators, build better relationships, and ultimately achieve better results. Whether it's used for personal development or to improve the performance of a team, NLP is a valuable tool for leaders looking to improve their skills and reach their goals.

Using NLP in personal development

Neuro-Linguistic Programming, or NLP, is a powerful tool for personal development and self-improvement. NLP is a set of techniques and methods that can help individuals understand and change the way they think, feel, and behave, allowing them to achieve their personal and professional goals more effectively. In this article, we will explore the various ways NLP can be used in personal development and the benefits it provides.

The first step in using NLP in personal development is to understand your own thoughts and behaviors. NLP techniques can be used to identify limiting beliefs, negative self-talk, and self-defeating behaviors that may be holding you back. For example, you may believe that you are not good enough, that you are not capable of achieving your goals, or that you are not deserving of success. These beliefs can be limiting and prevent you from reaching your full potential.

Once you have identified these limiting beliefs, NLP techniques can be used to change them. For example, you can use visualization and affirmations to reinforce positive beliefs and overcome negative self-talk. Additionally, NLP techniques such as anchoring and submodality changes can be used to create new, empowering beliefs that support your goals and aspirations. NLP can also be used to enhance communication skills and build stronger relationships. By understanding the way language affects thoughts and behaviors, you can use NLP techniques to influence and persuade others in a positive and ethical manner. This can be especially useful in business and leadership contexts, where the ability to communicate effectively is essential for success.

Another important aspect of personal development is setting and achieving goals. NLP can help you to clarify your goals, develop a plan of action, and stay motivated and focused on your progress. For example, you can use visualization and affirmations to help you stay focused on your goals and overcome any obstacles that may arise. Additionally, NLP techniques such as reframing and outcome-based thinking can be used to help you overcome self-doubt and maintain a positive, proactive mindset.

Finally, NLP can be used to help you overcome phobias, anxiety, and other emotional issues. NLP techniques such as desensitization and reframing can be used to help you overcome these challenges and develop a more positive and resilient mindset. By working through these issues and developing greater self-awareness and emotional intelligence, you can become more confident, self-assured, and capable of achieving your goals.

In conclusion, NLP provides a range of powerful techniques and methods for personal development and self-improvement. Whether you are looking to enhance your communication skills, build stronger relationships, achieve your goals, or overcome emotional challenges, NLP can help you to achieve your desired outcomes and reach your full potential. If you are interested in using NLP for personal development, consider seeking the guidance of a qualified NLP practitioner, who can help you to identify your goals and develop a customized plan of action.

Using NLP in Relationships

Neuro-Linguistic Programming (NLP) is a set of techniques and principles that can be applied to various areas of life, including relationships. NLP can help individuals understand and improve their communication with others, as well as develop a more fulfilling and satisfying relationship with their partners. Therefore, we will explore the use of NLP in relationships and how it can be applied to enhance the quality of our interactions with others.

One of the key principles of NLP is the idea that communication is not just about what is said, but also how it is said and the impact it has on the listener. This principle is particularly relevant in relationships, where clear and effective communication is essential for building trust and intimacy. NLP provides a framework for understanding the different ways that people communicate, including their preferred representational system, as well as their unconscious language patterns and habits.

Another key aspect of NLP is the use of rapport-building techniques, which are designed to create a sense of connection and mutual understanding between two people. In relationships, these techniques can help individuals establish a deeper level of trust and empathy with their partners, which can in turn lead to more open and honest communication. For example, NLP techniques such as mirroring and matching can be used to help individuals understand their partners' perspectives, emotions, and experiences.

NLP can also help individuals understand and manage their own emotions and thoughts, which can be particularly useful in resolving conflicts and improving the overall quality of their relationships. For example, NLP provides techniques for reframing negative thoughts and emotions, as well as for managing stress and anxiety in difficult situations. By learning to control their own thoughts and emotions, individuals can become more resilient and better equipped to handle the challenges that arise in relationships.

Another important aspect of NLP is the use of language patterns and techniques to influence and persuade others. In relationships, this can involve using persuasive language to negotiate and resolve conflicts, or to persuade a partner to see things from a different perspective. NLP techniques such as embedded commands and anchoring can also be used to help individuals create positive associations and build rapport with their partners.

In conclusion, NLP can be a powerful tool for improving relationships and enhancing the quality of our interactions with others. By understanding the principles and techniques of NLP, individuals can learn to communicate more effectively, resolve conflicts more easily, and build deeper, more fulfilling relationships with their partners. Whether you are looking to improve your personal relationships or your interactions with colleagues and clients, NLP provides a valuable set of tools and strategies for enhancing your communication skills and achieving your goals.

Disclaimer on using NLP as a Therapy or Coaching Technique

Neuro-Linguistic Programming (NLP) is a technique that has been used in various fields, including business, leadership, and personal development, among others. However, it is important to note that NLP is not considered a substitute for professional therapy or medical treatment. While NLP techniques may be useful for addressing certain emotional or psychological issues, they are not a cure for serious mental health problems or medical conditions.

In cases where individuals are experiencing severe symptoms, such as depression, anxiety, or obsessive-compulsive disorders, it is recommended that they seek the assistance of a licensed mental health professional. A mental health professional has the training and expertise to diagnose and treat these conditions using evidence-based methods and to provide support and guidance in a safe and confidential environment.

It is important to be cautious when using NLP techniques as a form of therapy, especially if the individual is not trained or experienced in using these techniques. Individuals who are untrained or inexperienced in using NLP techniques may not be able to accurately assess the situation or effectively apply the techniques, which could result in unintended consequences or harm.

Therefore, it is advisable to approach NLP as a complementary technique that can be used in conjunction with professional therapy or medical treatment, rather than as a standalone solution. In addition, it is important to be mindful of the ethical and legal considerations that may be associated with using NLP techniques, particularly in a therapeutic or coaching context.

In conclusion, NLP is a powerful and useful technique that has applications in various fields. However, it is important to approach it with caution and to seek professional guidance if necessary. If you are experiencing emotional or psychological distress, it is recommended that you seek the assistance of a licensed mental health professional.

Using NLP in Coaching

Neuro-Linguistic Programming (NLP) has been widely recognized as a powerful tool for personal and professional development, and coaching is no exception. NLP is an approach to communication and problem-solving that draws upon the links between language, thoughts, and behavior. This means that NLP provides a framework for understanding how we process information and make decisions, and how we can use this information to help people make changes in their lives. In coaching, NLP techniques are used to help clients understand their thoughts, emotions, and behaviors, and to facilitate change in those areas.

The first step in using NLP in coaching is to help the client become aware of their current state. This is done by encouraging the client to describe their thoughts, emotions, and behaviors in detail. NLP coaches use active listening and open-ended questions to help clients become aware of their current state, and to encourage them to describe their thoughts, emotions, and behaviors in a non-judgmental way.

Once the client has described their current state, the NLP coach can begin to use NLP techniques to help the client make changes. One common NLP technique used in coaching is the reframing of negative thoughts and behaviors. Reframing involves taking a thought or behavior that is having a negative impact on the client, and re-interpreting it in a positive way. This can help the client to change their perspective on a situation, and to begin to see it in a more positive light.

Another NLP technique that is commonly used in coaching is rapport building. Rapport building is about creating a relationship of trust and understanding between the coach and client. This can be achieved through non-verbal communication, such as mirroring the client's body language and tone of voice, and through the use of language patterns that are designed to build rapport and establish trust.

Another technique that can be used in NLP coaching is the use of anchoring. Anchoring involves creating an emotional or sensory association with a specific thought or behavior. This can be done through the use of physical touch, sounds, or other sensory stimuli. Once the anchor has been established, the client can be reminded of it whenever they need to make a change in their thoughts or behaviors. This can help the client to access positive emotions and thoughts, even in challenging situations.

NLP strategies are another important tool in NLP coaching. Strategies are sequences of thoughts, feelings, and behaviors that people use to achieve specific outcomes. By helping clients to understand their strategies, NLP coaches can help clients to identify areas in which they would like to make changes, and to develop new strategies to help them achieve their goals. Finally, NLP coaches often use techniques to help clients overcome limiting beliefs and emotions. Limiting beliefs are beliefs that hold people back and prevent them from achieving their goals. NLP coaches use techniques such as reframing and visualization to help clients overcome these limiting beliefs, and to develop a more positive outlook on life.

In conclusion, NLP provides a powerful set of tools and techniques for coaching, personal and professional development. By using NLP techniques such as rapport building, reframing, anchoring, and strategy development, NLP coaches can help clients to make positive changes in their lives, and to achieve their goals. NLP is a flexible and adaptable approach to coaching, and can be tailored to meet the needs of individuals, businesses, and organizations. Whether used in a personal or professional setting, NLP has the potential to make a positive impact on people's lives, and to help them achieve greater success and fulfillment.

Using NLP in Therapy

Neuro-Linguistic Programming (NLP) is a therapeutic approach that aims to help individuals overcome personal challenges, overcome limiting beliefs and behaviors, and achieve their goals. NLP combines the principles of neuroscience, linguistics, and programming to create an effective method for change. NLP has been applied in a variety of settings, including therapy, personal development, business, and coaching. In therapy, NLP can be used to help individuals overcome mental health issues, relationship problems, and other forms of personal difficulties.

One of the core principles of NLP is that our thoughts, feelings, and behaviors are interlinked, and that changing one can lead to changes in the others. For example, if an individual is struggling with low self-esteem, NLP can help them to identify the thoughts and beliefs that are causing this issue and then reframe them in a more positive light. By doing this, the individual can start to feel better about themselves, which in turn can lead to a more positive outlook and more empowering behavior.

Another important principle of NLP is that our experiences are filtered through our five senses, and that these experiences can be associated with positive or negative emotions. In therapy, NLP practitioners will often help individuals to access these sensory experiences and then modify them to create a more positive association. For example, if an individual has a traumatic experience that is associated with a particular smell, NLP can help them to change the way they respond to this smell so that it no longer triggers negative emotions.

One of the key techniques used in NLP is reframing, which involves looking at a situation from a different perspective in order to change the way it is perceived. For example, if an individual has a phobia of spiders, NLP can help them to reframe their thoughts about spiders so that they no longer feel fear. This can be done by identifying the underlying beliefs and attitudes that are driving the phobia and then changing them so that the individual has a more positive view of spiders.

NLP can also be used to help individuals to overcome limiting beliefs and behaviors. For example, if an individual has a belief that they are not good enough, NLP can help them to identify this belief and then challenge it by looking for evidence that contradicts it. By doing this, the individual can start to feel more confident and capable, which in turn can help them to achieve their goals and live a more fulfilling life.

NLP is also used in coaching and leadership to help individuals to achieve their goals and improve their communication and interpersonal skills. For example, NLP can help leaders to understand their own communication style and the communication styles of others, which in turn can help them to communicate more effectively. NLP can also help leaders to identify and overcome limiting beliefs and behaviors that are holding them back, and to develop a more empowering and effective leadership style.

In conclusion, NLP is a versatile and effective approach to personal development and therapy that combines the principles of neuroscience, linguistics, and programming to help individuals overcome challenges, achieve their goals, and live a more fulfilling life. Whether you are looking to improve your personal relationships, overcome mental health issues, or develop your leadership skills, NLP has something to offer. If you are interested in using NLP to improve your life, it is recommended that you seek out a qualified practitioner who can guide you through the process and help you achieve your goals.

Chapter 8

Advanced NLP Techniques

Reframing and Refocusing

Reframing and refocusing are two important concepts in the field of neuro-linguistic programming (NLP), which is a set of principles and techniques aimed at improving communication, personal development, and other areas of life. Reframing and refocusing are related concepts that involve changing the way we perceive, interpret, and respond to events, experiences, and emotions. By reframing and refocusing, individuals can change their thoughts, beliefs, and behaviors to achieve greater happiness, success, and fulfillment.

Reframing refers to the process of changing the meaning or interpretation of an event, experience, or emotion. This can be done by altering our perception of the situation or by re-evaluating the way we see it. Reframing can help individuals to reduce the impact of negative experiences, minimize the influence of limiting beliefs, and increase the impact of positive experiences. Reframing can also help individuals to see opportunities where they previously saw obstacles, and to find solutions where they previously saw problems.

For example, if an individual has a fear of public speaking, they might reframe that fear by telling themselves that they are excited to share their knowledge and experiences with an audience. Reframing the fear as excitement can change the individual's emotional response and make it easier for them to speak in public.

Refocusing refers to the process of redirecting one's attention away from negative experiences and emotions, and towards positive ones. Refocusing can be done by focusing on what is going well in one's life, or by setting goals and taking action towards achieving them.

Refocusing can help individuals to shift their focus from what they don't have, to what they do have, and to find gratitude and satisfaction in the present moment.

For example, an individual who is feeling overwhelmed by work may refocus by taking a few moments to meditate or practice deep breathing. Refocusing on the present moment and on their breath can help the individual to calm their mind, reduce stress, and increase focus and productivity.

In conclusion, reframing and refocusing are important concepts in NLP that can help individuals to change their thoughts, beliefs, and behaviors to achieve greater happiness, success, and fulfillment. By reframing and refocusing, individuals can reduce the impact of negative experiences, increase the impact of positive experiences, and find gratitude and satisfaction in the present moment. These techniques are simple, yet powerful, and can be easily integrated into one's daily life to improve communication, personal development, and other areas of life.

Parts integration and conflict resolution

Parts integration and conflict resolution is a key concept in Neuro-Linguistic Programming (NLP). The concept is rooted in the belief that individuals have multiple parts or sub-personalities within themselves, each with its own wants, needs, and motivations. When these parts are in conflict, it can lead to internal struggles, self-sabotage, and a lack of clarity in decision making.

In NLP, the goal of parts integration and conflict resolution is to bring these conflicting parts into harmony, enabling individuals to align their thoughts, behaviors, and emotions in support of their desired outcome. The process is typically achieved through a variety of techniques that help individuals identify, understand, and resolve internal conflicts.

One popular NLP technique for parts integration and conflict resolution is called the Parts Integration process. This technique involves guiding an individual through a structured process to identify their conflicting parts and bring them into harmony. The process typically begins with the individual imagining their conflicting parts as separate entities, and then having a conversation between these parts to understand their motivations and concerns. The goal is to bring the conflicting parts into agreement and to create a sense of unity and harmony within the individual.

Another NLP technique for resolving internal conflicts is Reframing. Reframing is the process of changing the way we think about a particular situation, person, or event. It involves looking at a situation from a different perspective, and finding a new interpretation that can lead to a resolution of the conflict. For example, if someone is feeling overwhelmed and stressed about a work project, reframing can involve shifting the focus from the challenges and difficulties to the opportunities and benefits of completing the project successfully.

Still another technique for resolving internal conflicts is called Time-Line Therapy. This technique is based on the idea that we store memories and experiences in a time-line, and that these memories can impact our current thoughts, behaviors, and emotions. In Time-Line Therapy, the individual is guided to locate the root cause of the conflict, and to release any negative emotions attached to the memories. This process helps the individual to clear their time-line, enabling them to move forward with greater clarity and confidence.

In conclusion, parts integration and conflict resolution is an important aspect of NLP. The goal is to bring conflicting parts into harmony, enabling individuals to align their thoughts, behaviors, and emotions in support of their desired outcome. The techniques used in NLP, such as Parts Integration, Reframing, and Time-Line Therapy, are effective ways to resolve internal conflicts and help individuals achieve greater clarity and success in their personal and professional lives.

Time-line therapy and future pacing

Time-line therapy and future pacing are two related NLP techniques that are used to help individuals overcome limiting beliefs, negative emotions, and unhealthy habits. These techniques involve accessing the unconscious mind and working with the internal representation of time to create a desired outcome. The goal of time-line therapy is to create a sense of empowerment and control over one's life, while future pacing involves imagining and rehearsing a desired future scenario to increase the likelihood of achieving it.

Time-line therapy is a powerful tool for resolving emotional and psychological issues that stem from past experiences. The technique assumes that people store their memories and experiences in a mental time-line, which is a representation of the linear progression of time. This mental time-line can be visualized as a line that stretches from the past to the present and into the future. By accessing this time-line, individuals can identify and release negative emotions that are tied to past events.

One of the key steps in time-line therapy is to locate the mental time-line and determine which direction it runs. Some people have a time-line that runs from left to right, while others have a time-line that runs from right to left. Once the direction of the time-line has been established, individuals can work to identify negative emotions that are tied to past experiences. These emotions may include anger, sadness, fear, guilt, or shame.

To release these negative emotions, individuals can use a technique known as "future-pull." This involves imagining the negative emotion moving away from the body and into the future. By visualizing this process, individuals can release the negative emotions and create a more positive outlook.

Future pacing is a technique that involves imagining and rehearsing a desired future scenario. This technique can be used to help individuals overcome limiting beliefs and increase their chances of achieving their goals. The idea behind future pacing is that by rehearsing a desired outcome, individuals can create a mental representation of it, which in turn makes it more likely to happen in real life.

To use future pacing, individuals first need to clearly define their desired outcome. This could be anything from achieving a specific goal to changing a particular habit. Once the desired outcome has been defined, individuals can imagine themselves experiencing it as if it has already happened. They can visualize all the sensory details, including what they see, hear, feel, and experience. By repeating this visualization, individuals can create a powerful mental representation of their desired outcome, which increases the likelihood of it becoming a reality.

In conclusion, time-line therapy and future pacing are powerful NLP techniques that can help individuals overcome limiting beliefs, negative emotions, and unhealthy habits. By accessing the mental representation of time and imagining desired outcomes, individuals can create a sense of empowerment and control over their lives, while increasing their chances of achieving their goals. These techniques are used in a variety of settings, including personal development, coaching, and therapy.

Chapter 9

Ethics and best practices

Ethical considerations in the use of NLP

Neuro-Linguistic Programming (NLP) is a powerful tool for personal and professional growth, but it's important to be aware of the ethical considerations when using it. NLP practitioners must adhere to a set of ethical principles that ensure they act in the best interests of their clients, respect their rights, and maintain the integrity of the field.

Here are some of the key ethical considerations in using NLP:

Informed consent: NLP practitioners must obtain informed consent from their clients before using NLP techniques. This means clients must be fully aware of what NLP is, what it involves, and what outcomes can be expected. They must also understand their right to refuse any NLP intervention and to withdraw their consent at any time.

Confidentiality: NLP practitioners must maintain client confidentiality, ensuring that they keep client information private and secure. This includes ensuring that they do not share information with unauthorized individuals, and that they dispose of client records appropriately.

Competence: NLP practitioners must be competent in the techniques they use, and must only use techniques that they have been trained in and are qualified to use. This means that they must stay informed about the latest developments in NLP and seek ongoing training and supervision to maintain their competence.

Responsibility: NLP practitioners must take responsibility for their actions and must avoid causing harm to their clients. They must act professionally and with integrity, and must be transparent about their methods and outcomes. They must also be aware of the limits of NLP, and recognize when clients may need to seek alternative forms of help.

Non-discriminatory practice: NLP practitioners must not discriminate against clients on the basis of age, gender, race, religion, or any other characteristic, and must respect the diversity of their clients.

Safety: NLP practitioners must ensure that their clients are safe during NLP interventions, and must avoid using techniques that could cause physical or psychological harm. They must also be aware of the effects of NLP on clients who may have a history of trauma or abuse.

Responsibility to others: NLP practitioners must be responsible to others in the field of NLP, and must not engage in practices that could damage the reputation of NLP or its practitioners.

Responsibility to society: NLP practitioners must act in the best interests of society and must not use NLP for unethical or illegal purposes.

By following these ethical considerations, NLP practitioners can help ensure that NLP remains a safe and effective tool for personal and professional growth, and that it is used in a responsible and ethical manner. It's important for practitioners to stay informed about the latest developments in NLP and to seek ongoing training and supervision to maintain their competence, and to always act in the best interests of their clients.

**Best practices for using NLP with clients and in
personal development**

Neuro-Linguistic Programming, or NLP, is a
powerful tool for personal and professional
development that can help individuals achieve
their goals and overcome obstacles. When used
properly and with consideration for ethical
principles, NLP can be a highly effective
approach for improving communication skills,
promoting personal growth, and enhancing
relationships. In this article, we will discuss
some of the best practices for using NLP with
clients and in personal development.
First and foremost, it is important to understand
that NLP is not a one-size-fits-all approach and
that every individual is unique. When working
with clients, it is essential to be open-minded
and non-judgmental, and to approach each
person with empathy and respect. This means
taking the time to understand the client's
perspective, identifying their goals, and tailoring
the NLP techniques to their individual needs.

Another key aspect of using NLP effectively is to be transparent and upfront about the process. Clients should be made aware of what they can expect from NLP, and how the techniques will be used to help them achieve their goals. This includes explaining the purpose of each exercise and what the client will be asked to do, as well as ensuring that they are comfortable with the process before proceeding.

In addition, it is important to establish clear boundaries and to respect the client's personal space. NLP techniques should never be used in a way that makes the client feel uncomfortable or violated, and it is crucial to be mindful of the client's physical and emotional well-being at all times.

Another best practice for using NLP with clients is to be flexible and adaptable. NLP techniques are not always effective for everyone, and it may be necessary to modify or adjust the approach in order to achieve the desired results. For example, some clients may prefer more structured exercises, while others may respond better to more creative, open-ended approaches. The key is to be flexible and to be willing to try different techniques until you find what works best for the individual.

When using NLP in personal development, it is important to be mindful of your own motivations and to approach the process with a positive, growth-oriented mindset. This means setting clear, achievable goals, and being willing to put in the effort and time required to achieve them.

It is also crucial to be patient and persistent in your personal development journey, as progress can sometimes be slow and difficult. However, by staying focused and motivated, and by using NLP techniques to help overcome obstacles and reframe limiting beliefs, individuals can achieve significant growth and improvement over time. Finally, it is important to seek out the guidance and support of an experienced NLP practitioner or coach when using NLP in personal development. A trained professional can help you identify your goals, provide guidance on the best techniques to use, and offer support and feedback as you progress.

In conclusion, by following best practices for using NLP with clients and in personal development, individuals can maximize the effectiveness of this powerful tool and achieve their goals. Whether working with a client, seeking personal growth, or using NLP to improve relationships, it is essential to approach the process with empathy, respect, and a positive, growth-oriented mindset.

Chapter 10

Conclusion

The study of neuro-linguistic programming (NLP) is a powerful tool for personal development and improvement in various fields, including business, leadership, relationships, coaching, and therapy. NLP is a model of communication and human behavior that is based on the idea that the way we think and experience the world is shaped by the way we use language and the five senses.

Throughout this course, we have explored the various components of NLP and how they can be applied to different aspects of life. The introduction to NLP provided an overview of the definition, history, and key principles of NLP, as well as the NLP communication model. The section on representational systems discussed the impact of the five senses on communication and how to identify and utilize a person's preferred representational system. The section on language patterns delved into the structure of language and how it affects thoughts and behaviors, and provided techniques for using language to influence and persuade others.

The section on anchoring explored the definition and explanation of anchoring, as well as techniques for creating and utilizing anchors. The section on submodalities covered the definition and explanation of submodalities, and provided techniques for modifying and altering submodalities to change thoughts and behaviors. The section on strategies discussed the definition and explanation of strategies, and provided techniques for identifying and utilizing strategies in communication and problem-solving.

The applications of NLP section explored the use of NLP in business and leadership, personal development and relationships, and coaching and therapy. The advanced NLP techniques section covered topics such as reframing and refocusing, parts integration and conflict resolution, and time-line therapy and future pacing. The final section on ethics and best practices discussed ethical considerations in the use of NLP and best practices for using NLP with clients and in personal development.

In conclusion, NLP is a comprehensive and versatile tool that can be used to enhance personal and professional development. Whether you are looking to improve communication skills, increase self-awareness, overcome limiting beliefs, or achieve specific goals, NLP can help. This course has provided a foundation for understanding the key concepts and techniques of NLP, and has given you the tools to continue your exploration and development in this field. By reviewing the key concepts and techniques learned, and using the resources for further study and development, you can continue to grow and expand your NLP skills and knowledge.

Skills that Complement NLP

Neuro-linguistic programming (NLP) is a valuable tool for personal growth, communication, and problem-solving. However, it is important to recognize that NLP is just one tool among many that can help individuals achieve their goals and improve their lives. There are a number of complementary skills and techniques that can enhance the effectiveness of NLP and provide additional benefits for individuals who use them. In this article, we will explore some of the skills that complement NLP and how they can be used together for maximum impact.

Emotional Intelligence

Emotional intelligence is the ability to recognize and understand our own emotions, as well as the emotions of others. It is a critical skill for effective communication and interpersonal relationships, and it complements NLP in several ways. By using NLP techniques to understand the emotions and perspectives of others, individuals can develop greater empathy and understanding, which can help them build better relationships and resolve conflicts more effectively.

Active Listening

Active listening is a critical skill for effective communication and problem-solving. It involves paying close attention to the words, tone, and body language of the speaker, and actively seeking to understand their perspective. This skill complements NLP by helping individuals gain a deeper understanding of the emotions, needs, and motivations of others, which can be used to build stronger relationships and resolve conflicts more effectively.

Conflict Resolution

Conflict resolution is a critical skill for success in both personal and professional relationships. It involves the ability to identify and resolve conflicts in a respectful and effective manner. This skill complements NLP by helping individuals understand the underlying emotions and perspectives of others, which can be used to resolve conflicts more effectively.

Mindfulness

Mindfulness is the practice of paying attention to the present moment, without judgment. It involves being aware of our thoughts, emotions, and physical sensations, and learning to observe them without becoming attached to them. This skill complements NLP by helping individuals gain a deeper understanding of their own thoughts, emotions, and physical sensations, which can be used to reframe negative thoughts and behaviors, and improve their overall well-being.

Goal Setting

Goal setting is a critical skill for success in both personal and professional life. It involves defining and prioritizing our goals, and taking action to achieve them. This skill complements NLP by helping individuals understand their own values, motivations, and desires, which can be used to set more meaningful and achievable goals.

Time Management

Time management is the process of planning and organizing how we spend our time to achieve our goals. It is a critical skill for success in both personal and professional life, as it helps individuals maximize their productivity and achieve their goals more effectively. This skill complements NLP by helping individuals understand the importance of setting priorities and allocating their time effectively, which can be used to improve their overall effectiveness and achieve their goals more efficiently.

In conclusion, NLP is a valuable tool for personal growth, communication, and problem-solving, and it can be enhanced by combining it with other complementary skills and techniques. By combining NLP with skills such as emotional intelligence, active listening, conflict resolution, mindfulness, goal setting, and time management, individuals can gain a deeper understanding of themselves and others, and improve their overall well-being, effectiveness, and success.

Thank you

It took me a long time to learn how to read and write when I was a child. Until the 5th grade I still struggled with spelling even simple words and my hand writing was worse. For those who will understand, I still haven't earned my "pen licence."

However, in time I learnt to read and write well enough to join the military and progress through university to pos graduate studies in psychology. For this there is two people I must thank. My grandmother Eliane Bultreys and my step grandfather Mike Miller.

Although it was painful as a child and into my teens, every time I was in the car with one of they would ask me to spell a word or read signs. Their persistence is what I owe the ability to read and write to, so thank you.